Exceptional
African Americans

LEBRON JAMES

Basketball Champion

E **Enslow Publishing**
101 W. 23rd Street
Suite 240
New York, NY 10011
USA

enslow.com

Charlotte Taylor
and
Stephen Feinstein

Words to Know

Cavaliers—The professional basketball team in Cleveland, Ohio.

community center—A place where people meet for activities or classes.

compete—To take part in a contest.

National Basketball Association (NBA)—The group of professional American basketball teams.

national tournament—A contest in which teams from the same country compete in a series of games.

rookie—A beginner; someone in his first year of playing in the NBA.

scouts—People hired by teams to look for their future players.

Contents

LeBron James

CHAPTER 1

The Christmas Gift

One of the first Christmas gifts LeBron James ever received was a toy basketball set. Even though he was only three years old, LeBron knew just what to do with it. He grew up to be one of the greatest basketball players of his time.

LeBron James was born on December 30, 1984, in Akron, Ohio. His mother, Gloria, was only sixteen and still in high school. LeBron never knew his father. Gloria and LeBron lived with Gloria's mother, Freda.

LeBron Says:

"Before anyone ever cared where I would play basketball, I was a kid from northeast Ohio. It's where I walked. It's where I ran....It holds a special place in my heart."

A Sad Time

On Christmas Eve 1988, LeBron's mother was looking forward to the next day. She had bought a toy basketball set for LeBron, who was almost four. But Christmas Eve turned out to be very sad. Later that night, LeBron's grandmother, Freda, suddenly died. She had been very sick, but nobody else knew.

LeBron loved to play basketball. He started when he was three years old, just like this little boy.

LeBron grew up in the poor neighborhoods of Akron, Ohio.

The next day, LeBron opened his Christmas presents. His mother had decided not to tell him about his grandmother until after Christmas. When LeBron saw the basketball and hoop, he went wild. Gloria watched in amazement as the little boy ran up to the hoop and dunked the ball.

CHAPTER 2

Hard Times

After LeBron's grandmother died, he and his mother had to move. They went to stay with friends because they did not have their own home. They were very poor.

When LeBron was five, he and his mother moved seven times in one year. Sometimes they lived in the housing projects, apartment houses for poor people. Sometimes there were gang fights there. Gloria and LeBron were always scared about what was going to happen next.

A Difficult Choice

LeBron never stayed in one school very long. He often missed school because he had no way to get there. When LeBron was in the fourth grade, he missed eighty-two days of school. Gloria loved LeBron, but she wanted a better life for him. She had to make a difficult decision. She sent LeBron to live with Frankie Walker and his family.

Frankie was a basketball coach at the **community center**. LeBron had gone to the center to learn how to play basketball. Frankie taught LeBron new moves. LeBron learned very quickly. He learned how to shoot, how to control the ball, and how to play defense. But LeBron would learn much more than just basketball from Frankie and his family.

Like these boys, Lebron loved playing basketball when he was young.

LeBron Says:

"Basketball is my passion. I love it. But my family and friends mean everything to me. That's what's important."

CHAPTER 3

Shooting Stars

Everything changed when LeBron moved in with the Walker family. He had chores to do and rules to follow. In the fifth grade, he did not miss a single day of school, and his grades were good. Things were looking up.

LeBron joined a basketball team called the Shooting Stars. He became close friends with three boys on the team: Dru Joyce, Jr.; Sian Cotton; and Willie McGee. The four friends called themselves the Fab Four.

A Big Win

LeBron never missed a basketball practice, and he kept getting better. The Shooting Stars went to a **national tournament** in Salt Lake City, Utah. Teams from all over the country came to **compete**. LeBron played as hard as he could to beat the other teams. The Shooting Stars won first place. LeBron was named the Most Valuable Player of the tournament. The Shooting Stars later went on to win more than two hundred games.

LeBron Says:

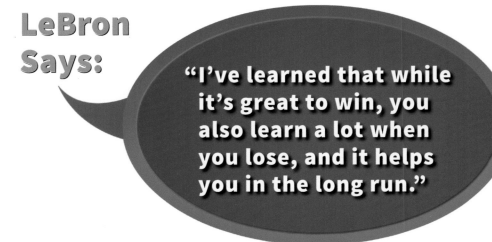

"I've learned that while it's great to win, you also learn a lot when you lose, and it helps you in the long run."

The Fab Four wanted to keep playing basketball together. So in 1999, the four friends entered Saint Vincent-Saint Mary (SVSM) High School in Akron. LeBron led the SVSM team, the Fighting Irish, to one championship after another. In 2001, LeBron was named Ohio's "Mr. Basketball," the top high school player in the state.

Growing up, LeBron's favorite basketball player was Michael Jordan.

CHAPTER 4

LeBron Rises to the Top

LeBron was already famous at his high school. But soon people from all across the country knew his name. During his third year at SVSM, **scouts** from the **National Basketball Association**, or NBA, came to watch him play. He was the best high school player they had ever seen. LeBron was fast, strong, and very tall: six feet, seven inches. LeBron could jump high enough to dunk the ball through the hoop. People began calling him "King James."

During his last year at SVSM, LeBron's picture was on the cover of *Sports Illustrated* magazine. He was now famous. But LeBron still worked hard at basketball practice. Every day he shot nearly eight hundred jump shots. LeBron also worked hard at his schoolwork. He always got good grades.

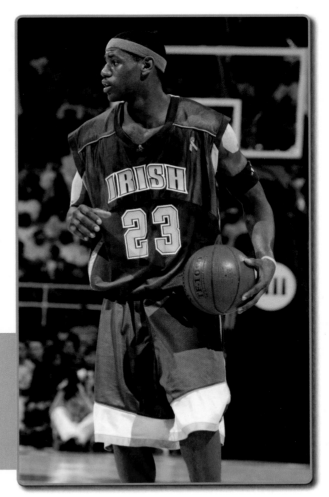

Lebron played for the Fighting Irish in high school.

A New Job

LeBron graduated from high school in the spring of 2003. He was picked by the Cleveland **Cavaliers** to play on their team. Wherever the Cavaliers played, crowds came to see LeBron. For the 2003–2004 season, LeBron was named **Rookie** of the Year, the best first-year player in the NBA.

LeBron has had the chance to play for his country in three Olympic Games. In 2004, he won a bronze medal as a member of the US Men's Basketball Team. In 2008 and 2012, he helped his team win the gold medal.

The Move to Miami

In 2010, LeBron made a difficult choice. He left the Cavaliers to join the Miami Heat. Many of his fans were angry. But LeBron had to do what was right

Kevin Durant, LeBron James, and Russell Westbrook stand for the National Anthem at the London 2012 Olympic Games.

LeBron has fun playing basketball with a group of children.

for him. In 2012 and again in 2013, he helped his team win the NBA championship.

Being on a championship team was something LeBron had always wanted. But in 2014, he announced that he was going back to the Cavaliers. He now has a new goal—to win a championship with the Cavaliers. When he is not playing basketball, LeBron spends a lot of time helping kids in need. On and off the court, LeBron hopes to show young people that they should never stop reaching for their dreams.

LeBron Says:

"Ask me to play. I'll play. Ask me to shoot. I'll shoot...But it's not what you ask of me. It's what I ask of myself."

Timeline

1984—LeBron James is born in Akron, Ohio, on December 30.

1999—LeBron enters Saint Vincent-Saint Mary High School (SVSM) in Akron, Ohio.

2001—LeBron is named Ohio's "Mr. Basketball."

2002—LeBron appears on the cover of *Sports Illustrated* magazine.

2003—LeBron graduates from high school and is picked to play for the Cleveland Cavaliers.

2004—LeBron wins a bronze medal as a member of the US Olympic Basketball Team.

2006—LeBron is voted Most Valuable Player (MVP) in the NBA All-Star Game.

2007—LeBron helps Cleveland defeat the Milwaukee Bucks, 104–99. He is the youngest player to score 9,000 career points.

2008—LeBron wins a gold medal as member of the US Olympic Basketball Team. He earns his first NBA MVP award.

2009—LeBron earns his second NBA MVP award.

2010—LeBron leaves the Cavaliers for the Miami Heat.

2011—LeBron earns his third NBA MVP award.

2012—LeBron wins his second gold medal with the US Olympic Basketball Team. He wins his first NBA Championship with the Miami Heat. He earns his fourth NBA MVP award.

2013—LeBron marries Savannah Brinson. He wins his second NBA Championship with the Heat.

2014—LeBron announces he is returning to the Cavaliers.

Learn More

Books

Bodden, Valerie. *LeBron James: Champion Basketball Star.* Edina, Minn.: ABDO, 2014.

Morreale, Marie. *LeBron James.* New York: Children's Press, 2014.

Norwich, Grace. *I Am LeBron James.* New York: Scholastic, 2015.

Web Sites

lebronjames.com

Learn about LeBron's background, charity work, and basketball news.

jockbio.com/Bios/James/James_bio.html

Detailed biography of LeBron James.

nba.com/playerfile/lebron_james/bio.html

Includes statistics, biography, and video clips.

Index

Published in 2016 by Enslow Publishing, LLC.
101 W. 23rd Street, Suite 240, New York, NY 10011

Copyright © 2016 by Enslow Publishing, LLC.

Library of Congress Cataloging-in-Publication Data
Taylor, Charlotte, 1978-
   LeBron James : basketball champion / Charlotte Taylor and Stephen Feinstein.
      pages cm. — (Exceptional African Americans)
   Includes bibliographical references index.
   Summary: "A biography of basketball player LeBron James"—Provided by publisher.
   ISBN 978-0-7660-6660-1 (library binding)
   ISBN 978-0-7660-6658-8 (pbk.)
   ISBN 978-0-7660-6659-5 (6-pack)
   1. James, LeBron—Juvenile literature. 2. Basketball players—United States—Biography—Juvenile literature. 3. African American basketball players—Biography—Juvenile literature. I. Feinstein, Stephen. II. Title.
   GV884.J36T39 2015
   796.323092—dc23
   [B]
                                 2015007445

Printed in the United States of America

To Our Readers: We have done our best to make sure all Web site addresses in this book were active and appropriate when we went to press. However, the author and the publisher have no control over and assume no liability for the material available on those Web sites or on any Web sites they may link to. Any comments or suggestions can be sent by e-mail to customerservice@enslow.com.

Photo Credits: Getty Images: Damian Strohmeyer/Sports Illustrated, pp. 1, 4; Boston Globe, p. 11; Sporting News Archive/Sporting News, p. 17; Jeff Haynes/AFP, p. 15; Christian Petersen/Getty Images Sport/Getty Images Europe, p. 19; Philippe Lopez/AFP, p. 20; Shutterstock.com: © Toria (blue background): pp. 1–3, 5, 9, 13, 16, 22–24; © Flashon Studio, p. 7, © Henryk Sadura, p. 8; © Lane V. Erickson, p. 12.

Cover Credits: Damian Strohmeyer/Sports Illustrated/Getty Images (portrait of LeBron James); ©Toria/Shutterstock.com (blue background).